W9-AMA-770

NFL ★ TODAY

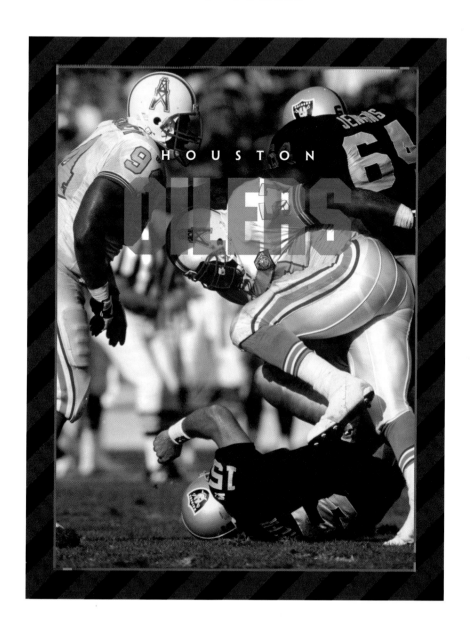

HOUSTON OILERS

MICHAEL GOODMAN

CREATIVE EDUCATION

7977481

Published by Creative Education
123 South Broad Street, Mankato, Minnesota 56001
Creative Education is an imprint of The Creative Company

Designed by Rita Marshall
Cover illustration by Rob Day

Photos by: Allsport Photography, Associated Press, Bettmann Archive,
Duomo, Focus on Sports, FPG International, Sissac, and SportsChrome.

Copyright © 1997 Creative Education.
International copyrights reserved in all countries.
No part of this book may be reproduced in any form without written
permission from the publisher.
Printed in the United States of America.

Library of Congress Cataloging-in-Publication Data

Goodman, Michael E.
Houston Oilers / by Michael Goodman.
p. cm. — (NFL Today)
Summary: Traces the history of the team from its beginnings through 1996.
ISBN 0-88682-810-4

1. Houston Oilers (Football team)—History—Juvenile literature.
[1. Houston Oilers (Football team)—History. 2. Football—History.]
I. Title. II. Series.

GV956.H68G66   1996   96-15237
796.332'64'097641411—dc20

123456

Television and movies have given us an image of Texas as a "big" state. Everything is bigger there: bigger hats, bigger cars, bigger ranches. And for sports fans in Texas, nothing is bigger than their love for professional football. In Houston, the biggest city in Texas, the team the fans love best is the Houston Oilers.

The Oilers began their history somewhat like an outlaw in a cowboy western. The club's founder and owner, K.S. "Bud" Adams, sought permission in the late-1950s to put a National Football League franchise in Houston. When the established league turned him down, however, he helped to form the

American Football League to compete against the NFL for players and fans. Ten years later, a successful Houston franchise finally joined the NFL as part of a merger of the two leagues.

For more than 35 years, the Oilers have been noted for a special brand of hard-driving and high-flying football played by offensive standouts such as George Blanda, Billy Cannon, Earl Campbell, Dan Pastorini, Ken Burrough, Warren Moon, Drew Hill and Ernest Givins; and tough, hard-hitting defensive stars like Elvin Bethea, Curley Culp, George Webster, Robert Brazile and Jim Norton.

In the 1990s, new talents emerged including Steve McNair, Gary Brown, Darryll Lewis, Mark Stepnoski, Rodney Thomas and Chris Sanders. The Oilers are ready to gush to the top of the league again.

Double duty! Billy Cannon led Houston in both rushing and punt returns.

STARTING OUT ON TOP

It is fitting that the history of the Houston Oilers is closely tied to the fortunes of a Texas oil man—Bud Adams. Adams lettered in football in both high school and college. World War II and success in the oil business deflected Adams away from a pro career, but he never lost his love for the sport.

Adams was one of the first people whom fellow Texas oil man Lamar Hunt contacted in 1959 about buying a team in the new AFL that would start play the following year. Adams was given the task of attracting football fans in south Texas to the new Houston franchise.

Nothing came easy to the Oilers at first, but almost everything turned out right for them. First, the team selected halfback Billy Cannon, the Heisman Trophy winner from Louisiana

6   *Allen Pinkett was a leading kick returner (page 7).*

1 9 6 1

Lucky Seven!
Quarterback George
Blanda threw for
seven touchdowns
in a single game.

State University, as its first college draft pick and even signed him on the field of the Sugar Bowl on January 1, 1960. Then the NFL's Los Angeles Rams produced a similar contract signed by Cannon. The two teams went to court over the matter, and a judge ruled in Houston's favor. Cannon went on to star in Houston for four years and continued his solid playing career in Oakland.

A second bit of luck for the Oilers involved signing quarterback George Blanda before the 1960 season. Blanda, who was both a passer and a placekicker, had an up-and-down career with the Chicago Bears from 1949 to 1958. Then he was traded to the Baltimore Colts, who wanted him solely as a kicker. Blanda balked at that idea and retired, sitting out the 1959 season. Oilers coach Lou Rymkus went to Blanda and convinced the signal-caller that someone with his competitive fire should be playing football every week and not watching it. The challenge appealed to Blanda, and he began a new career in the AFL, at age 33, that lasted until he was nearly 49. Seven of those years Blanda played in Houston, leading the Oilers to first-place finishes in the AFL's Eastern Division during the league's first three seasons and to league championships in both 1960 and 1961. After setting pro records for most seasons played (26), most games played (340) and most points scored (2,002) in a career, Blanda was inducted into the Pro Football Hall of Fame in 1981.

The Oilers' one significant setback in their early years involved finding a suitable place to play their home games. The only available site was Jeppesen Stadium, a local high school field, which the club renovated to bring its seating capacity up to 36,000. The shabby surroundings did not attract fans at first, but the club's outstanding play soon did. By the end of the 1960 season, over 32,000 people packed into Jeppesen to see the Oilers defeat the Los Angeles Chargers 31-23 to capture the first-ever AFL championship. Billy Cannon was named the game's MVP, and each Houston player received a winner's share of $1,016.42.

The following year, Adams helped to get an $18 million bond issue passed to finance the building of the Harris County Domed Stadium, better known as the Houston Astrodome. The Oilers finally moved into the "domed wonder" in 1968. But while they were waiting, they continued to provide an exciting brand of football for Houston fans.

Grand theft touchdown! Ken Houston scored four TDs on interceptions during the season.

The Oilers continued atop the AFL standings in both 1961 and 1962. In 1961, the club got off to a slow start and then ran off ten wins in a row. Along the way, Houston became the first team in pro football history (NFL or AFL) to tally over 500 points in a season. The Oilers ended the year with a narrow 10-3 victory over the Chargers, but it was good enough for a second straight AFL title.

In 1962, Houston kept up its offensive attack, led by Blanda's passing to flanker Charley Hennigan. For the third consecutive year, the club reached the AFL championship game. This time, the Dallas Texans (soon to become the Kansas City Chiefs) found a way to stop them, but it took a field goal in double-overtime to end the Houston winning streak.

THE OILERS' ROLLERCOASTER RIDE

That loss to Dallas seemed to be an omen of bad things to come for the Oilers. Houston suffered through its first

Dan Pastorini (#7) ran the offense throughout the '70s (pages 10-11).

1 9 7 3

Elvin Bethea set a team record with 17 quarterback sacks.

losing season in 1963 and then began a strange rollercoaster ride up and down the standings over the next 11 years, from 1964 to 1974. During the period, the Oilers had seven losing seasons, three seasons ending in .500 records and one glorious winning campaign when they came within a game of reaching the Super Bowl.

Why the Oilers performed so unevenly is hard to explain, especially since they had four of football's finest athletes during this period. These were performers who, under better conditions, might have led their teammates to the Super Bowl.

Defensive lineman Elvin Bethea joined the Oilers in 1968 out of North Carolina A & T. Bethea played 16 seasons and 210 games with the Oilers, both club records. He was fast and tough, leading the club in quarterback sacks in six different seasons. He is also one of only three Oilers whose jersey numbers have been retired by the club.

While Bethea terrorized opposing quarterbacks with his fierce rushes, linebacker George Webster and safety Ken Houston drove them crazy with outstanding coverage of receivers near the line of scrimmage and downfield. Both men joined the Oilers in 1967 and had an immediate impact, helping to turn a team that had finished in last place in 1966 into a division leader. The Oilers reached the AFL championship game in 1967, but could not overcome the powerful Oakland Raiders to win a berth in Super Bowl II.

Webster and Houston continued to star in the league long after their rookie seasons. Webster was later named to the All-Time AFL Team by a special selection committee. Houston, a Pro Bowl player for an amazing 12 consecutive seasons, was inducted into the Pro Football Hall of Fame in 1986. That was a pretty impressive accomplishment for a player who admitted that he took up football in high school mainly to impress the girls. "I wanted a girlfriend," he later recalled, "and it seemed that only the football players had girlfriends."

Tall, handsome quarterback Dan Pastorini won the hearts of both girlfriends and football fans during his playing days at Santa Clara College and with the Oilers. He came to Houston as a number one draft pick in 1971. The Oilers didn't have much of an offensive line during Pastorini's first few seasons in Houston, so he spent much of his time trying to escape from onrushing linemen. He also got a lot of work as the team's punter when Oilers offensive drives stalled. But by 1975, Pastorini was ready for big things, and so were Oilers fans.

1 9 7 5

Bum Phillips led the Oilers to a 10-4 record in his first season as head coach.

"BUM" AND "THE TYLER ROSE"

Despite fine individual performances by players such as Bethea, Webster, Houston and Pastorini, the Oilers had lacked the leadership and direction to become an outstanding team. That was about to change with the elevation of defensive coordinator O.A. "Bum" Phillips to head coach before the 1975 season. During the next six years under Phillips, the Oilers would record five winning seasons, win two divisional crowns and reach the AFC championship game twice. They would also pack the Astrodome week after week with rabid fans wearing the team's light blue and white colors and waving "Luv Ya Blue" banners.

It wasn't just his success as a football coach that endeared Phillips to Houston fans. His unique nickname and unusual style of dress on the gridiron—ten-gallon Stetson hat, lizard or

1 9 7 8

Rookie Earl Campbell was magic as he led the league in rushing with 1,450 yards.

snakeskin boots and a plaid Western shirt—also grabbed the public's attention.

Declaring that a little shakeup would be good for the Oilers, Phillips began the rebuilding process right away with the 1975 college draft. With Houston's first three picks, he selected linebacker Robert Brazile of Jackson State, Texas A & I running back Dan Hardeman and Kansas wide receiver Emmett Edwards. He worked all three men immediately into Houston's starting lineup with positive results. Brazile, nicknamed "Dr. Doom" because of his hard tackles, was selected All-Pro in 1975 for the first of seven consecutive years. Hardeman became one of the club's leading rushers, and Edwards joined veteran wide receivers Ken Burrough and Billy "White Shoes" Johnson as targets for Dan Pastorini's passes.

Phillips' "new" Oilers opened up 6-1 in 1975 and finished with a 10-4 record, their first winning season since 1967. The big surprises for the year were Brazile's poise and leadership ability as a rookie, the Pastorini-to-Burrough passing combination that accounted for over 1,000 yards and eight touchdowns, and the amazing play of Billy Johnson, who tied a league record by returning four kicks (three punts and one kickoff) for touchdowns during the season.

Despite the Oilers' initial success under Phillips, it wasn't until 1978 that Houston really began climbing to the top of the league. The prize plum that Bum Phillips plucked in the draft that year was the incomparable Earl Campbell from the University of Texas. In seven seasons as an Oiler (1978-84), Campbell would win four NFL rushing titles, set nearly every club running record, and be selected by his fellow NFL players as the Jim Thorpe Award recipient for Most Valuable Player three consecutive years (1978-80).

Linebacker Robert Brazile was an All-Pro in the 1970s.   15

1 9 7 9

Speedy receiver Billy "White Shoes" Johnson averaged 18 yards per catch for the Oilers.

Campbell's outstanding play eventually earned him a place in the Hall of Fame, yet his football prospects were not very bright in his childhood. "The Tyler Rose" (his nickname in college) had grown up in tiny Tyler, Texas. Attracted to pool, cigarettes and whiskey, he seemed destined for jail. After he was shot in the leg during a drunken brawl, however, the young Campbell decided to put all of his energy into football. Thus began one of the game's great success stories.

Campbell's high school and college records only hinted at what his pro career would be like. NFL fans got their first glimpse of his greatness during a nationally-televised Monday Night Football game on November 20, 1978. In that game, Campbell personally dismantled the favored Miami Dolphins, scoring four touchdowns and rushing for 199 yards in a 35-30 Houston victory.

"What you have seen tonight," sportscaster Howard Cosell shouted after Campbell scored on an 81-yard run in the fourth quarter, "is a truly great football player taking personal command of a game."

Campbell took command of lots of other games, too. He did it with an awesome mixture of power, speed and determination. "I liked to run through people," Campbell explained. "Anybody can run around them. I never said much as a player. I was real low-key, but I was really cocky on the inside. I didn't think there was anything I couldn't do on a football field. And I had more fun out there than anyone could imagine."

Houston fans had lots of fun, too, cheering for a revitalized Oilers squad. Behind Campbell and Pastorini on offense and Bethea and Brazile on defense, the Oilers reached the playoffs in 1978 for the first time in nine years. They came from

The powerful Earl Campbell. 17

In his last year with Houston, quarterback Dan Pastorini threw for 14 touchdown passes.

behind in the Wild Card game to defeat Miami again, 17-9, then crushed New England 31-14 to reach the AFC championship game against the Pittsburgh Steelers. There, a slippery, rain-soaked field and a smothering Pittsburgh defense did in the Oilers, 34-5, and ended their hopes of reaching the Super Bowl.

The same two teams battled in the AFC championship game the next year as well—with the same result. Pittsburgh went on to win a second straight Super Bowl title, while the Oilers went home once again without reaching their goal.

Bum Phillips decided to pull out all of the stops in 1980 in an effort finally to win it all. In a controversial trade, Phillips sent Pastorini to Oakland for veteran quarterback Ken Stabler. Stabler had Super Bowl experience, but also an aging arm and bad knees.

Yet the trade seemed to work out. Stabler passed for over 3,200 yards—more than Pastorini ever had in one year—and handed off to Campbell for nearly 2,000 more yards. The result was an 11-5 record and a third straight playoff berth. The Oilers couldn't get past their playoff jinx, however. In a sad homecoming for Stabler, the Raiders trounced the Oilers 27-7 to knock Houston out of the playoffs once again.

As it turned out, Houston lost more than a game that day. In a post-game press conference, Bum Phillips admitted that his team had been "outplayed and outcoached" by Oakland. While that may have been an honest and accurate judgment, team owner Bud Adams saw Phillips as a defeatist. Furious at his coach's remarks, Adams fired him two weeks later.

Letting Phillips go proved to be one of Adams' worst decisions. During the next four seasons, the Oilers went through three coaches and, in their worst year, sank to a 2-14 record. The core of the team was changing. The offense was decimated by the departures of Stabler and Burrough in 1981 and Earl Campbell's increasingly weak knees. The defense also began to suffer when Elvin Bethea retired in 1983 and Robert Brazile called it quits the following year.

Former Oilers defensive coordinator Jerry Glanville took over as head coach.

Houston's decline was finally halted in 1985, when assistant coach Jerry Glanville took over as head coach. Glanville set his sights on returning Houston to the playoffs, but he knew that would take work. As Glanville graphically stated in an interview, "When I came here in '84, we had the nicest guys in the NFL. Their mamas loved 'em. Their daddies loved 'em. But they couldn't hit if you handed them sticks." He wanted to turn the Astrodome into a "House of Pain," a place where visiting teams would feel the power of the Oilers' exciting offense and the force of their crushing defense.

Glanville's task of turning the Oilers into winners again was made easier due to the presence of quarterback Warren Moon, who had joined the Oilers in 1984. Moon, an All-American at the University of Washington, had chosen to play in the Canadian Football League rather than in the NFL after leaving college. He played six seasons with the Edmonton Eskimos, leading the club to the CFL's Grey Cup championship five straight years

Warren Moon invested ten years with the Oilers.

(1978-82) and establishing himself, in Glanville's words, as "the best quarterback in football." He certainly proved he had one of the strongest right arms of all time when, in 1982 and 1983, he passed for more than 5,000 yards and connected for 36 touchdowns each year. The next year, Hugh Campbell, Moon's former coach in Edmonton, convinced him to come south to continue his sterling career in Houston.

Campbell's stay in Texas was short-lived, but Moon revolutionized the Oilers' offensive attack for ten seasons under coaches Jerry Glanville and Jack Pardee. By the time he moved on to Minnesota after the 1993 season, Moon had established Houston records for career passing yardage, attempts, completions and touchdowns. But he couldn't set those records alone. Moon needed top receivers to catch his rifle shots, and Glanville brought in such standouts as Drew Hill, Ernest Givins and Haywood Jeffires. That amazing trio caught over 1,500 passes during their years in Houston.

Glanville also focused on rebuilding the Oilers defense. Drafting players such as defensive end Ray Childress and cornerbacks Richard Johnson and Cris Dishman, and trading for linemen William Fuller and Sean Jones, Glanville laid the foundation for his "House of Pain" squad. Houston fans loved the tough new team and began showing up at the Astrodome in record numbers once again. Houston's opponents, on the other hand, hated to come to the Astrodome now. Several coaches challenged Glanville to fights after games, claiming that he had taught his squad to "play dirty."

Whatever Glanville was teaching his players, it seemed to work. Starting in 1987, the Oilers reached the playoffs seven straight seasons. But getting there was one thing; getting to the Super Bowl was another. Houston lost in the second round in

Defensive end Ray Childress was a leader of the Oilers' dominating defense.

Left to right: Warren Moon, Alonzo Highsmith, Mel Gray, Rich Camarillo.

both 1987 and 1988. In 1989, a first-round overtime defeat to Pittsburgh, 26-23, ended Houston's year early once again.

That loss prompted Bud Adams to fire Glanville and to turn the team over to former NFL linebacker Jack Pardee, who had previously coached both the Chicago Bears and Washington Redskins to winning records.

1 9 8 9

Running back Mike Rozier gained 301 yards and averaged 3.4 yards per carry.

Pardee decided to combine the club's best weapons—Warren Moon's speed and quick release of the ball and the receiving ability of Hill, Givins, Jeffires and Curtis Duncan—to create a new kind of offensive attack: "the run-and-shoot." Most of the Oilers' new plays revolved around Moon's scrambling out of the pocket formed by the offensive linemen and finding one of his receivers streaking across or down the field. The results were remarkable. Moon completed 766 of 1,239 passes over the next two years (62 percent) for 9,379 yards and 56 touchdowns. Yet his passing arm continued to misfire in the playoffs, as the Oilers fell to Cincinnati 41-14 in the first round in 1990 and succumbed to Denver 26-24 in the second round in 1991.

But even those losses couldn't prepare Oilers fans for the bitter ending to the 1992 season. That year, Houston went into Buffalo's War Memorial Stadium as an underdog in the AFC Wild Card game but roared out to a 35-3 lead early in the third quarter. Moon couldn't seem to miss that day, and the defense led by Ray Childress and Bubba McDowell looked unbreakable. Then an evil spirit seemed to take over the game. Combining touchdown passes from quarterback Frank Reich with daring onside kickoffs, Buffalo staged the greatest comeback in NFL history to take a 38-35 lead late in the fourth quarter.

Leonard Harris holds the ball under a Patriots crush (pages 26-27).

Quarterback Chris Chandler hopes to return from injuries and recover his star passing form.

Still, the Oilers weren't through. Moon rallied his troops for one more drive, which ended with an Al Del Greco field goal to tie the contest with 12 seconds to go and send it into sudden-death overtime. Houston won the toss and took the opening kickoff. But Moon threw an interception, and a face-mask penalty on the return of that interception gave Buffalo the ball deep in Houston territory. Three plays later, the defeat was sealed by a Buffalo field goal for a 41-38 win.

The downhearted Oilers rallied once more in 1993, winning their last 11 games of the season to achieve the best record in their history, 12-4. Yet the year ended up the same as the previous six—with a playoff loss.

PREPARING FOR THE FUTURE

It seemed clear to most Oilers fans, and certainly to Bud Adams, that some changes were needed. In 1994, Houston willingly allowed Warren Moon to leave as a free agent, despite the gap his departure left in the Oilers' attack. By mid-season, when the injury-riddled team was 1-9, Pardee was fired in favor of assistant coach Jeff Fisher. Fisher finished out a disappointing 2-14 campaign, one of the worst marks in team history, and then began planning a major rebuilding effort.

The key to the Oilers' future is the man the club selected first in the 1995 NFL draft—quarterback Steve McNair from Alcorn State. While he had a great college career, McNair never faced high-level competition at Alcorn State. Some football experts have doubts about his ability to become a big-time pro quarterback, but not Bud Adams. "He's our most exciting draft choice since Earl Campbell," the team owner commented. "Drafting Earl turned our franchise around. Signing Warren Moon turned

Few AFC rookies outshined running back Rodney Thomas.

Receiver Haywood Jeffries was a dangerous force in the 1990s.

Placekicker Al Del Greco was a steady scoring threat.

Running back Eddie George, drafted out of Ohio State, is destined to become a star.

us around again. I see Steve McNair doing the same thing. You don't win a Super Bowl without a quarterback to lead the team, and I think Steve's the guy to do it."

"I know what they expect of me," McNair said after his selection, "but I don't think there is too much pressure on me because of it. I like to win, and that's what keeps me going. Hard work is the mark of a champion, and I'll work as hard as I can to help the Oilers."

McNair did most of his hard work at the beginning of the 1995 season in practice. During games he usually sat on the bench and watched veteran Chris Chandler try to get the team moving. Near the end of the season, however, with the club floundering below .500, Fisher decided to see what McNair could do in a game situation. McNair impressed his coaches by leading Houston to solid wins over the New York Jets and the Buffalo Bills in the final two games of the year.

Two other rookies also made impressive debuts during the 1995 season: running back Rodney Thomas from Texas A & M and wide receiver Chris Sanders from Ohio State. Thomas gained 947 yards on the ground to lead all rookie rushers in the AFC. His total included a spectacular 74-yard touchdown jaunt against the Denver Broncos. Sanders quickly became the club's scoring threat through the air, grabbing five touchdown tosses during one three-game stretch in mid-season.

Lots of faces have changed in Houston recently. Now what must change is the club's luck in the playoffs. The team that won AFL championships in the first two years of its history is ready for its first Super Bowl title, too. Now, that would make really "big" news in Texas.